Invest in Luxury

Insights for Wealth Growth through Luxury Goods

Table of Contents

Chapter 1. Introduction

Welcome to "Invest in Luxury: Insights for Wealth Growth through Luxury Goods", a special report designed for the investor who dreams in Technicolor, appreciates victory like a rare Bordeaux, and seeks wealth as ardently as connoisseurs seek out the finest timepieces. Our affluent voyage unlocks the gilded doors of investment opportunities in the luxury goods sector, taking you through a radiant journey of sparkling diamonds, sleek supercars, haute couture, and exquisite artworks. Journey with us as we reveal secrets of high-end markets, decode trends, and provide keen insider perspectives on how to broaden your wealth with the lustrous allure of luxury goods. Luxury isn't just a lifestyle, it also carries the potential for momentous profitability. Snap up this special report today and let us guide you through the lucrative path of investing in life's finer things! Discover the joy of investing with style, and make your wealth not just grow, but glow!

Chapter 2. Understanding the Landscape of Luxury Goods

Investing in luxury goods spans across a diverse range of industries, from fashion to high-end automobiles, alcohol to timepieces - each showcasing its own set of trends, consumer behaviors, and profit margins. Understanding this landscape requires familiarizing oneself with the macroeconomic factors that influence these markets, the idiosyncrasies of each luxury product category, and the buying patterns that shape demand.

2.1. The Macroeconomic Factors

Numerous macroeconomic factors build the foundation of any investment, and luxury goods are no different. However, luxury investments stand unique with their depiction of purchasing power and economic stability.

Global economies play a fundamental role in shaping the luxury market. The countries boasting the most luxury consumers include the United States, China, Japan, and European nations like France, Italy, and the United Kingdom. The interplay of these economies offer pertinent trends in the luxury goods market. For instance, a boom in Western economies in the 1990s spurred the growth of the luxury goods market globally, while the Japanese financial crisis in the late 1990s resulted in a slowdown of luxury sales in Asia, a trend that reversed with China's rapid growth in the new millennium.

Often branded as 'aspirational purchases', the demand for luxury goods increases with the rise in disposable incomes, mass affluence, and overall wealth of a society. The growing middle classes in emerging markets like India, China, and Brazil have spurred on the demand for luxury brands.

It's also noteworthy how luxury goods sales are affected by global geopolitical events. Brexit uncertainties, for example, temporarily boosted luxury goods sales in the UK due to the resulting weaker pound, which attracted foreign luxury buyers. On the flip side, luxury goods industries take a hit during periods of political instability and economic slowdown, such as during the 2008 financial crisis or amidst pandemics.

2.2. Luxury Product Categories

Investors attempting to understand the landscape of luxury items should become well-versed in the various product categories involved. These categories include fashion and leather goods, high-end automobiles, fine wines and spirits, watches and jewelry, and luxury hospitality services.

Fashion and Leather goods: Top-tier fashion labels like Gucci, Louis Vuitton, and Chanel dominate this segment, valued for their craftsmanship, design, and long-lasting quality. Handbags made from expensive materials like snake or crocodile skin, or even diamonds are eye-catching investment pieces.

High-end Automobiles: Luxury automobiles, particularly classic models from marques like Ferrari, Mercedes, and Rolls Royce, are seen as appreciating assets and can offer notable returns. Recent years have seen a surge in the market for electric luxury cars, championed by Tesla.

Fine Wines and Spirits: Investment portfolios aren't just about stocks and bonds anymore. High-quality wines and spirits, particularly from renowned vineyards, have seen growing interest from investors. A bottle of vintage wine can appreciate considerably over time.

Watches and Jewelry: High-end watches from brands like Rolex, Patek Philippe, and Audemars Piguet, as well as jewelry from renowned houses like Tiffany and Cartier hold their value over time, and in many cases increase in value due to their limited production and growing demand.

Luxury Hospitality Services: This sector encompasses high-end hotels, resorts, and travel services that offer unique and opulent experiences. While not a tangible good, a profitable portfolio in this sector can demonstrate value appreciation.

2.3. Luxury Buying Behaviors

Understanding consumer behavior is crucial when investing in any market. In the world of luxury goods, a combination of brand loyalty, quality expectation, and aspiration shapes the demand curve.

Brand Loyalty: Luxury consumers are often loyal to specific brands, which have built their reputations over years, even centuries, of meticulously crafted products and carefully-constructed branding.

Quality Expectation: Luxury consumers expect the highest quality from their purchases. This demand for perfection continues to drive brands into crafting superior products, often made with exotic, high-cost materials and artisans' fine skills.

Aspiration: Luxury has traditionally been seen as a sign of success and a symbol of social status. Many consumers aspire to own luxury goods as a way to mark their success. This aspiration can lead to continued demand even during economic downturns, as luxury goods are often seen as investment belongings that can hold or increase their value over time.

To summarize, the landscape of luxury goods takes us through the world's wealthiest economies, introduces us to high value tangible assets and dives into the minds of luxury consumers. Understanding these elements is essential in making informed investment decisions in the luxury goods market.

While the landscape of luxury goods may seem vast and complex, the pillars that hold it - the macroeconomic environment, the product categories, and the luxury consumer, provide a sturdy base on which a thriving investment portfolio can be built. As we delve into the complex world of luxury goods investing, remember that each piece of knowledge gained paves the way to potentially lucrative investments. Your wealth not just grows, but glows, when you invest in luxury.

Chapter 3. Decoding the Patterns: Trends Shaping Luxury Markets

Every industry has its eye on the ebb and flow of current and emerging trends to gain a competitive edge. In the realm of luxury goods, keeping a finger on the pulse of the market's dynamics is a golden key to success. This chapter deciphers the trends that are shaping luxury markets and offers insight into the patterns of consumer behavior that savvy investors need to know.

3.1. Understanding Luxury Consumer Behavior

Luxury consumer behavior is distinct, significantly impacted by socio-cultural shifts, economic outlook, technology advancements, and changing demographics. The luxury consumer of today is far from one-dimensional. They demand extraordinary quality, exclusivity, heritage, and the ability to provide them with meaningful experiences.

A recent trend we've observed has been a shift towards 'conspicuous consumption.' This practice happens where consumers purchase expensive items to display wealth and income rather than to cover their real needs. It's intricately tied to the consumers' desire for social status and recognition. Take, for example, the surge in popularity of exclusive designer handbags or limited-edition timepieces, often acting as signals of success and belonging to a particular social status.

But along with conspicuous consumption, we are also witnessing a simmering trend of conscious consumption. Driven by a new breed of high-net-worth individuals, this sees consumers favor brands that prioritize sustainable practices, ethical sourcing, and social responsibility. Luxury brands cannot afford to ignore their environmental footprint if they are to appeal to this growing demographic.

3.2. The Impact of Technology on Luxury Goods

Technology is another force to reckon with in the luxury goods market. Digital innovation has brought new channels for reaching consumers and reshaped the retail experience as a whole.

E-commerce and online shopping have made luxury products more accessible than ever, resulting in the democratization of luxury. Brands can now reach potential consumers through social media advertising, email marketing, and other digital platforms.

However, luxury brands can't solely rely on digital interactions. The human touch, personalized service, and the tactility of luxury products are still critical. Thus, we see a trend towards 'phygital' experiences – blending physical and digital aspects to offer a truly immersive, unique, and tailored buying experience.

Another area where technology is creating waves is in the realm of product authentication. With the rise of the resale luxury market, validating the authenticity of the product has become increasingly critical. Technologies like blockchain and AI are being utilized for this, providing a more trustworthy and secure customer experience.

3.3. Changing Market Demographics

The rise of wealthy millennials and Generation Z, along with the continued affluence of Baby Boomers, are key demographic trends redefining the luxury market. These groups have distinct attitudes towards luxury, with younger cohorts demanding unique experiences and personal expressions.

The Asian market, particularly China, is also becoming significantly important in the luxury landscape. Propelled by a booming middle class and high-net-worth individuals, the appetite for luxury goods in Asia is skyrocketing. However, with this new opportunity comes challenges of cultural understanding and localization, adding another layer of complexity for luxury brands.

3.4. The Future of Luxury: Experience Over Ownership

Increasingly, luxury consumers seek experiences that don't just promote ownership, but also provide uniqueness, enrichment, and grandeur. Hence, luxury travel, fine dining, and well-being experiences are gaining traction. This shift has far-reaching implications, fundamentally altering the form and substance of luxury products and services.

In conclusion, monitoring and adapting to these multi-dimensional trends will set successful investors apart in the future. A keen observer can differentiate between passing fads and lasting market shifts, making their venture not just about investing in luxury, but a luxurious investing journey of its own. Be it silverware or stocks, may your discernment be as sharp as it is indulgent.

Chapter 4. The Art of Investing in Art

Art investing immerses one in the vibrant world of tangible beauty and creativity while potentially yielding significant financial returns. Unlike traditional markets, art investment transcends mere numbers and graphs—it allows investors to experience a nuanced matrix of history, culture, passion, and economics.

4.1. Understanding the Art Market

The art market operates on different principles from standard businesses and financial endeavors. Its main entities are artists, collectors, art dealers, auction houses, and art advisers. Each offers different perspectives and plays unique roles in the art investment landscape.

Artists create works that spawn an entirely new asset class, while collectors, driven by personal passions or monetary gain, fervently amass unique pieces. Art dealers facilitate transactions and often act as intermediaries between artists and collectors. Auction houses provide a public platform for art sales, and art advisers offer independent advice on acquiring and disposing of art.

Understanding the difference between primary market (first sale of artwork from artists) and secondary market (subsequent sale or resale of artwork) is crucial for investors. In the primary market, prices are often lower, and investments riskier, as the value of emerging artists can be volatile. Conversely, the secondary market deals with well-known artists with well-established values, making it safer but often more expensive.

4.2. Key Investment Factors Within Art

Art investment is inherently subjective, which is why understanding key value determinants can be fruitful:

1. Artist's Reputation: Works by famous artists typically veer into astronomical price ranges. Names like Picasso, Van Gogh, and Warhol carry commanding weight, significantly influencing the artwork's value.

2. Rarity: As with luxury goods, scarcity drives desire. A rare piece by a revered painter or sculptor can be worth a fortune.

3. Provenance: The documented history of an artwork, including past owners and exhibition history, impacts the art's value greatly. Works with a rich, traceable provenance generally fetch a higher price.

4. Condition: Preservation hugely affects an artwork's value. Damage or alteration can dramatically reduce its worth.

4.3. Navigating Auctions and Galleries

Many art transactions happen at auctions or galleries. Auctions offer a public, transparent buying process where demand directly meets supply. However, they can also be intense, leading to rapid price escalation.

Art galleries, on the other hand, offer a more relaxed, contemplative buying experience, with prices decided by the dealer or artist rather than the market. Investors should thoroughly research ahead of time and consult with trusted advisers to negotiate the best deals.

4.4. Measuring Art Performance

There is no universal standard for gauging art investment performance due to the uniqueness and variability of art as an asset class. The Mei Moses Art Indices and the Blouin Art Sales Index are two popular tools that track returns based on repeated sale pairs of artworks. However, investors should exercise caution as these tools are based on historical data and might not predict future performance.

4.5. Art as a Diversifying Asset

An advantage of art investment lies in its low correlation with traditional assets like stocks and bonds. This makes art a potent diversifying tool in a well-curated investment portfolio. Though the rate of return may not always match equities over the long term, it typically exhibits less volatility, providing a measure of stability during financial turbulence.

4.6. Risks in Art Investment

Art investment is not without its perils. Aside from the highly subjective nature of artwork valuations, the art market lacks liquidity, and the selling process can be slow and uncertain. The risk of forgery or theft, high transactional costs, and maintenance expenses for art pieces are other factors potential buyers should consider.

4.7. Conclusion: Making Art Work for You

Art investment intertwines aesthetic pleasure with financial gains, making it a captivating and potentially lucrative venture. However, it's more than just buying a painting or sculpture — it's about understanding market dynamics, appreciating art, and managing risk. It's a journey in which your investment portfolio becomes a gallery, each piece a testament of your savvy in navigating the radiant world of art and the monetary realm alike.

Embrace these intricacies, and the art market can yield handsome rewards, financial and otherwise. So begin your journey, explore the galleries, and converse with artists. Immerse yourself in the symphony of color, shape, and imagination, and let art work wonders for your wealth. Investing in this visually vivid market isn't just about amassing riches; it's about forming a profound connection with human creativity and expression. It's not solely an investment, it's an adventure.

Chapter 5. The Gleam of Investing in Jewelry and Precious Gems

Ancient civilizations prized precious gems and jewelry for their beauty and the wealth they symbolized. Today, this sentiment still holds strong and jewelry, particularly those encrusted with diamonds, rubies, emeralds, and various precious gems, continue to mesmerize with their timeless allure. More than just accessories to accentuate outfits or showcase wealth, these extravagant pieces have solidified their place in the world of investments.

5.1. Understanding the Basics

When we discuss jewelry as an investment, it's crucial to differentiate between high-end and low-end jewelry. Low-end or commercial jewelry, typically found in malls or chain jewelry stores, is unlikely to appreciate in value over time. However, high-end jewelry, crafted with exceptional workmanship and often adorned with high-quality diamonds or gemstones, tends to retain, if not exceed, its original value over time.

Similarly, not all precious gems yield the same investment potential. Diamonds, rubies, emeralds, and sapphires are often touted as the four most investing-worthy gems due to their hardness, rarity, and consistent demand in the market.

5.2. Navigating the Marketplace

Before one can embark on a lucrative adventure in the gem and jewelry sector, it's essential to understand its global scope and interconnected nature. Operational levels span from mining and production to design and retail. In addition, the marketplace is marked by multi-tiered networking, dealing with raw materials, loose stones, or finished jewelry pieces.

The marketplace has recently seen a surge in online trading platforms and digital auctions, opening doors towards greater transparency, convenience, and reach. It's encouraged a place for competitive pricing while also attracting a younger, tech-savvy demography.

5.3. Evaluating the Investment

To effectively evaluate the potential return on investment, it is imperative to understand the fundamentals of pricing for precious gems and jewelry. Key factors influencing the value include the rarity and quality of the gemstones, the weight of precious metals, along with the design and craftsmanship.

Special emphasis should be given to gemstones. In the case of diamonds, one refers to the 'Four Cs'—color, clarity, cut, and carat. For colored gems, color, clarity, cut, and carat weight are considered, but other factors such as origin and treatment can also impact the price.

It is also advisable to consider the piece's provenance and whether it's a product of a renowned designer or luxury brand. Branded pieces usually fetch higher prices, due in part to the intrinsic value of the brand name.

5.4. Building a Collection

Building a collection of precious gems and jewelry can be a remarkable journey, but it should be embarked upon with careful planning and an investment strategy. Match your purchases to your personal style as well as financial aspirations. Remember, timing is also key; the best times to buy are often when the economy is more robust, and the gems or jewelry artefacts can then be sold when the economy dips and traditional assets underperform.

Diversifying across different gems, styles, and eras can help balance risks and could lead to better eventual returns. Also, consider working with trusted jewelers or consultants who can help navigate the high-end market trends.

5.5. The Impact of Contemporary Trends

Contemporary trends play a pivotal role in the world of precious gems and jewelry investments. Current trends point towards a rising demand for colored stones, ethical sourcing and sustainable mining practices, as well as pieces that tell 'a story' or carry sentimental value.

Despite downsides, investing in jewelry and precious gems adds an aesthetic dimension to your portfolio, combining financial returns with the joy of owning beautiful, timeless pieces. A carefully assembled collection can serve not only as a safety net in uncertain times but also as a source of pride and enjoyment for years to come.

Remember, investing in precious gems and luxury jewelry isn't simply about quick financial returns, but about embracing the long game, savoring the touch of luxury these pieces bring while backing their steady appreciation over time. Use knowledge of the market, trends, and individual pieces to make informed decisions, ensuring your investments shine as brightly as the precious pieces themselves.

With the right advice, a keen eye, patience, and a bit of luck, even gems can grow alongside your wealth. Combining the thrill of owning magnificent gems and jewelry with the stable, tangible investment they represent, this sector certainly shines with irresistible charm and potential.

Chapter 6. From Runways to Wealth: Profit Potentials in High Fashion

The essence of high fashion, the essence of haute couture lies not only in the stitching of high-quality materials into designs but also in its ability to create wealth. High fashion, tantamount to investing in art, can yield significant financial returns, and justly holds a powerful sway on the balance sheets of so many savvy investors. The following analysis delves into the cornerstone dynamics of haute couture as a luxury investment market, pinpointing profitable trends and opportunities.

6.1. The Economics behind High Fashion

As with any investment, understanding the fundamental economics lays the groundwork for successful strategies. High fashion remains a thriving sector within the luxury goods market, which by itself has grown by almost 50% over the past decade, accruing a total worth now nearing $1.5 trillion globally. The high fashion industry pulls from a diverse revenue stream, encompassing not just dress sales, but licenses, accessories, perfumes and cosmetics, and even homeware. Luxury brands that straddle these multiple sectors offer a unique investment portfolio themselves.

The rarity and exclusivity attached to haute couture items act as underpinnings for their value. Each piece is bespoke, handmade, and tailored to a specific customer's measurements, rendering it a unique and valuable artifact. Still, while the main goal of high fashion designers remains creating wearable art, these thoughtful designs transform into investible commodities, treated akin to a Rembrandt masterpiece or a Patek Phillipe timepiece.

6.2. Spotting Investment Avenues in High Fashion

Luxury brands like Gucci, Chanel, and Prada have become synonymous with high fashion, commanding superior cachet when referencing prestige and style. With avenues for investment lying in both brand's equity and the acquisition of haute couture items, the two work synergistically to offer a diversified approach to fashion industry investing.

When considering equity investments, one major advantage lies in the existence of business conglomerates like Kering and LVMH, which respectively own brands such as Gucci, Yves Saint Laurent, Louis Vuitton, and Dior. Buying into conglomerate-owned businesses allows investors an opportunity to invest indirectly in several brands whose performances influence the stock prices.

On the other hand, acquiring individual pieces of haute couture can be both a matter of personal enjoyment and an investment strategy. Like art, the price of high fashion appreciates with age. Condition, rarity, relevance to current trends, and provenance contribute to the item's value over time.

6.3. Investment Risks and Risk Mitigation Strategies

Investing in high fashion isn't without its risks— trends change, brands rise and fall, and the overall global economic climate can significantly impact the value of your investment.

Notably, high fashion is considerably volatile as a sector, with trends often influencing brand reputation and, by implication, stock prices.

More importantly, knock-offs and the growing acceptance of counterfeit products within certain economies forms a significant challenge.

Investors diversifying their fashion portfolio can mitigate such risks. Paying attention to brands' track records, their reputation for quality, innovation, and the management of their financial health are factors to consider before investing. From a collector's standpoint, insurance or secure storage options can protect the value of collected pieces.

6.4. Trendspotting and Selection

Success in the fashion investment world is closely tied with an investor's ability to gauge trends. Following fashion weeks globally can offer insights into upcoming trends and predict the popularity (and potential profitability) of particular styles, designers, or brands.

Keeping up-to-date with who's who in fashion and what their positions mean in the broader market is also invaluable. Fashion-focused resources like Vogue Business bring the investor fashionable insight and analysis, enabling them to keep abreast of industry movement.

6.5. The Longevity of the Investment

As with any investment, patience is necessary when creating a strategy for high fashion. Over the past two decades, we've borne witness to the increasing value of iconic brands, with pieces from the likes of Hermès and Chanel often worth more ten years after their initial purchase. Such instances underline the asset characteristics of high-fashion pieces, but these usually require a nurturing eye and a long-term time horizon.

In conclusion, investing in high fashion—whether through equity or by collecting pieces—provides a unique opportunity for wealth creation. With a nuanced understanding of the fashion world and an ability to stay ahead of the curve, savvy investors can turn the runway into a path toward accumulated wealth. The allure of high fashion extends beyond just its aesthetic – it holds the possibility of reaping hefty financial benefits. Approach it with the eye of a connoisseur and the rigor of an investor – and let your wealth model the style!

Chapter 7. Adding Sparkle to Your Portfolio: Watch and Jewelry Investments

In the world of luxury investments, watches and jewelry have played a pivotal role, capturing the passion of collectors and investors alike. Their exquisite design and enduring value sets them apart from conventional investment products, and adds an undeniable touch of elegance to your financial portfolio.

7.1. Assessing the Value of Watch and Jewelry Investments

Watches and jewelry have long held their place in the world of high-end collectibles. While a stunning timepiece or an exquisite piece of jewelry is always a welcome addition on a personal aesthetics level, discerning investors also understand their potential as tangible assets.

When assessing the investment value of watches and jewelry, several key factors come to play: Brand heritage, rarity, condition, and the presence of precious stones or metals.

Internationally recognizable brands such as Patek Philippe, Rolex, and Audemars Piguet have built their reputation over the centuries, and their timepieces usually hold, or even appreciate, in value. Similarly, heritage jewelers like Cartier, Tiffany & Co., Graff, and Harry Winston create pieces that not only enchant with their beauty, but also hold strong investment value.

Rarity also plays a prime role. Limited-edition watches, or jewelry pieces boasting rare gemstones like blue diamonds or untreated rubies, often command higher resale values due to their unique appeal.

The condition of a watch or a piece of jewelry significantly impacts its value too. Pieces in near-mint or mint conditions are naturally more sought-after and will fetch better prices.

Then, there is the matter of intrinsic value. Watches and jewelry made with gold, platinum, or encrusted with valuable gemstones carry inherent worth from these precious materials.

7.2. Research Before Investing

As with any investment, buying luxury watches and jewelry requires due diligence. Stay up-to-date with industry updates, learn about different brands and models, and understand market trends and price fluctuations. Collectors' forums, watch fairs, auction previews and post-sale reports provide rich sources of information.

When making an acquisition, it's also essential to have a reputable watchmaker or gemologist verify the piece's authenticity and condition. This helps to avoid overvaluation, or worse, counterfeit pieces.

7.3. Understanding Risks

As tangible assets, luxury watches and jewelry carry risk factors different from traditional financial instruments. While there is potential for significant gains, there are also possibilities of loss. Depreciation over time, market volatility, and difficulty in finding buyers are all real concerns.

For this reason, it is recommended to view watch and jewelry investments as long-term pursuits. The best investment pieces are often those that have withstood the test of time and market flux.

7.4. Portfolio Diversification

In order to mitigate risks, diversify your investment portfolio. Spread your investments across different brands, styles, and eras. Consider investing in both contemporary and vintage pieces.

7.5. Buying from Reputable Sources

Always purchase from reputable sources to ensure authenticity. Trusted retailers, well-respected auction houses, or recognized online platforms provide piece of mind and often additional buyer protection. Always demand for the original box and documentation, verifying the item's provenance and ownership history.

7.6. The Art of Selling: Timing and Venue

Selling luxury watches and jewelry, much like buying, requires strategy and understanding of the market. Timing is crucial – release of new models, celebrity endorsements, and brand anniversaries can all cause price fluctuations. The selling venue matters too - private collectors, auction houses or online platforms each have their benefits and drawbacks to consider.

Investing in luxury watches and jewelry demands engagement and passion, but the rewards can be gratifying both aesthetically and financially. Holding a physical representation of your investment offers an enjoyment that few other investment avenues can match. With the right choices and well-paced strategies, these additions to your portfolio can indeed bring sparkle not just to your collection, but to your wealth accumulation journey as well.

Chapter 8. Taste the Good Life: Investing in Fine Wine and Spirits

The enduring allure of fine wines and spirits has always been founded on the premise of their appreciating value, coupled with the joy they bring to the senses. As a potential investor in this field, you'll find that the rich tapestry of flavors available in the wine and spirits market allow you to enjoy your investments in a sensory fashion unlike any other investment avenue.

8.1. The Wine and Spirits Market: A Quick Primer

Before delving into the details of investing in fine wines and spirits, it is helpful to understand the basic composition and trends within the market. Fine wines command a premium price due to factors such as rarity, age, production team, region, and brand reputation. While fine spirits, including aged whiskies, vintaged rums, and exclusive cognacs, also appreciate value based on similar factors, their market mechanism is somewhat different and often more volatile due to higher demand sensitivity.

The global market for wine and spirits has seen consistent improvement over the years, driven by rising affluence and refinement of tastes in emerging economies, as well as a renaissance of appreciation for craft spirits and fine wine in established markets like North America and Europe.

8.2. Tips for Starting a Fine Wine Collection

Starting off an investment foray into wines can be intimidating, with diverse regions, grape types, and vintages to choose from. However, few invaluable tips and a systematic approach can make the process easier and more rewarding.

1. Learn about major wine regions: Classic regions include Bordeaux and Burgundy in France, Piedmont and Tuscany in Italy, and Napa Valley in California, among others. The character, flavor profiles, and investment potential of wines significantly differ between these regions.

2. Start with common vintages: These are excellent for beginners and can help familiarize you with different taste profiles and wine styles. Make sure to store these correctly, as they may appreciate over time.

3. Work with a trusted merchant or consultant: Their knowledge and connections can prove invaluable when building your collection.

8.3. The Art and Science of Wine Storage

Proper storage is critical in maintaining and potentially enhancing the value of your wine investment. Key factors to consider are stable cool temperature (around 12-15 degrees Celsius is often recommended), little to no light, high humidity (around 70% relative humidity), and good ventilation.

Consider investing in a wine fridge or a professional wine storage facility, especially for higher-end wines. It's also recommended to buy wines in their original case, which can increase their value compared to loose bottles.

8.4. Investing in Fine Spirits

Fine spirits can offer more immediate returns on investment compared to wine due to their shorter maturation and bottling periods. However, this asset is also more susceptible to market fluctuations, making due diligence equally important.

Among spirits, single malt whisky from Scotland (particularly from regions such as Islay, Highlands, and Speyside), bourbon from America, and cognacs from France are the most sought-after by collectors and investors. Rare and limited releases, older expressions, and spirits from closed distilleries generally command high prices at auctions.

8.5. The Power of Patience and Diversification

Much like traditional forms of investment, a successful portfolio of fine wines and spirits should be well-diversified and held onto patiently to allow value appreciation.

This may involve diversifying your investments across different types of wines (red, white, rose, sparkling), different regions (e.g., French, Italian, Californian, Australian), and different vintages. Similarly, your spirits portfolio can be diversified by including a mix of whiskeys, bourbons, and cognacs, among others.

Patience is another indispensable trait for successful investing in this field. It's advisable to hold onto your bottles for a few years to allow their value to appreciate. Rare bottles, in particular, may take years, even decades, to reach their peak value.

In conclusion, investing in fine wine and spirits offers an intoxicating mix of sensory satisfaction, historical richness, and potential for financial gains. As with any other form of investing, it requires careful study, a discerning palate, and an understanding of the market dynamics. However, if pursued with patience, passion, and a pinch of adventurousness, it may indeed prove to be one of the most rewarding investment endeavors, providing returns that not only accrue in your bank account but also delight your senses.

Chapter 9. The High Rollers: Profiting from Luxury Automobiles

Automobiles have always represented more than just a mode of transportation - they are a statement of prestige, power, and personality. The luxury automobile sector is no different. It is a realm of stunning aesthetics, exceptional performance, and technological brilliance. Here, iconic brands such as Bentley, Ferrari, Porsche, and Rolls-Royce reign supreme, their models reflecting an epitome of automotive craftsmanship and extravagance. Indeed, when considering investing in luxuries, high-end automobiles present an enticing opportunity with appreciable returns for the discerning investor.

9.1. The Luxury Automobile Sector: An Overview

The luxury automobile industry is a multifaceted galaxy of opportunities for investment. This sector represents the higher end of the automotive industry, where cars are not just vehicles but works of art with cutting-edge dynamics, unprecedented comfort, and breathtaking design. While the global auto industry is vast, the luxury segment forms a robust dynamic that offers significant investment potential.

Luxury car manufacturers have mastered the art of branding, and their marques are associated with status, making them extremely desirable. Even during economic downturns, luxury car sales have shown resilience, reflecting the non-cyclical nature of demand among the affluent consumer base. In fact, according to a report from Allied Market Research, the global luxury car market size was valued at $495.7 billion in 2018, and is projected to reach $733.2 billion by 2026.

However, the thrill of investing in luxury cars isn't merely in sales of new vehicles. Value can appreciate over time, especially in relation to classic and collectible cars. According to the Knight Frank Luxury Investment Index, classic cars have appreciated in value by 288% over the past decade.

9.2. Delving Deeper: Classic Cars

Classic automobiles are a tangible asset class that has outperformed many traditional investment sectors in the past decade. The uniqueness, rarity, and heritage associated with classic cars have made them particularly desirable to investors and collectors alike.

Investing in classic cars is not as straight forward as buying stocks or bonds. It requires understanding the factors that contribute to value appreciation, such as provenance, rarity, historical importance, and condition. Collectible automobiles, particularly models from marques like Ferrari, Aston Martin, and Jaguar, have consistently seen impressive value appreciation.

There are numerous avenues to invest in classic cars, including auctions, direct purchases, and even classic car funds. Attending Concours d'Elegance events and automobile shows can offer excellent opportunities to meet other collectors and build a network that can lead to investment opportunities.

9.3. Supercars: The Beacon of Luxury's Future

Supercars represent the pinnacle of automotive engineering and luxury. Brands such as Lamborghini, Bugatti, and McLaren release limited-edition models that often sell out before they even hit the production line, offering significant investment potential.

For instance, the McLaren F1, initially released in 1994 at a price of around $1 million, is valued at upward of $15 million currently. The limited production numbers coupled with the demand from wealthy clientele lead to such astronomical value appreciations.

One caveat with investing in supercars is understanding the market's proclivities. Not every super expensive or limited-edition car will appreciate in value. It takes a keen understanding of the market and often consultation with experts to make informed investment decisions.

9.4. The Role of Electric Luxury Automobiles

The evolution of the luxury car market is moving hand-in-hand with innovations in automotive technology. Electric Vehicles (EVs) have shown promise in carving out a significant niche within the luxury sector. High-end EVs blend the allure of clean energy with luxury, and manufacturers like Tesla are redefining what luxury automobiles can be.

Investing in high-end electric vehicles requires understanding the rapid changes in technology and consumer preference. The potential is enormous - the global electric vehicle market size was valued at $162.34 billion in 2019. It also pays to understand the nuances of charging infrastructure, government policies, and incentives that might impact the investment return.

9.5. Conclusion

The potential for growth and returns from luxury car investments is monumental, and the charm is irresistible. However, like any other investment, it is essential to thoroughly research before diving in.

This involves understanding current trends, historical appreciation, the factors leading to valuation, and above all, developing a genuine passion for these magnificent machines. A well-informed approach combined with an appreciation for luxury cars lays a strong foundation for successful and satisfying investments.

By aligning wealth growth ambitions with the lustrous allure of luxury automobiles, not only might investors make prudent financial decisions, but also live out their passion for these timeless marvels. Luxury car investing, when executed well, isn't just about monetary gains - it's the joy ride of a lifetime.

Chapter 10. Cruising Towards Fortune: Insights into the Luxury Yacht Market

Bronzed by the Mediterranean sun, gleaming under the soft lights of Monaco, yachts are symbolic of opulent living and a luxurious lifestyle. Not just an accessory for rich, holidays and leisure, but they also offer investors the opportunity to achieve significant returns. A deep dive into the world of luxury yachts reveals a thriving market, shaped by changing demographics, technological advancements, and evolving consumer preferences.

10.1. The Fleet and the Fortune

Luxury yacht fleet size has been steadily increasing over the past decade. As per Boat International's Market Intelligence report, the worldwide luxury yacht fleet has seen a substantial increase. This growth in fleet size has simultaneously charted the path for increased returns on investment.

Some may invest in luxury yachts for personal use, while many others look at it as a leasing opportunity. The charter business continues to demonstrate robust growth with a burgeoning demand for luxury yacht vacations. Millennials with high disposable income are more inclined towards experiencing luxury rather than owning it, driving the market for leased yacht vacations. The high-end clientele's ever-changing desires for unique experiences make the luxury yacht market dynamic and profitable.

10.2. Understanding the Investment Prospects

Investing in luxury yachts involves a sound understanding of the associated prospects and challenges. There are two primary routes to investment. Firstly, purchasing a yacht for personal use, which can also be chartered when not in use to generate revenue. The latter model is one of investment in a charter yacht, where the investor profits from its rental income.

In the world of luxury yachts, depreciation is seldom a concern as the true luxuries never fall out of fashion. The notion is especially true for custom-built yachts from reputable shipyards, which often maintain high resale values over time. Moreover, a well-maintained yacht can demonstrate a positive ROI, given the increasing charter rates, which tend to offset the operating costs.

10.3. Ascending the Waves of Market Trends

In the words of Bob Dylan, "The times they are a-changin'," and so are the trends in the luxury yacht market. Sustainable engineering and technology are playing an increasingly pivotal role with growing environmentally-conscious clientele. Carbon-neutral yachts and hybrid propulsion systems are redefining the market.

Design trends are also evolving with a lean toward minimalism, multifunctionality, and personalization. Incorporation of wellness spaces such as spas, gyms and cinemas has become essentially integral. Luxury yacht designers and architects now closely collaborate with purchasers to build custom floating homes tailored to their taste.

10.4. Sailing through Market Pitfalls

Like the tranquil sea that hides depth and danger, the luxury yacht market also presents inherent risks. These may include fluctuating currency exchange rates, regulatory laws, operating expenses, and certain unanticipated costs like repairs and maintenance. Thorough research and professional advice are imperative for navigating through these potential challenges.

10.5. Conclusion

The luxury yacht market is a combination of pleasure and profitability. The ongoing technological innovations and changing market trends render it an exciting sector for potential investors. With a careful understanding of the market and expert advice, it offers considerable returns and an opportunity to be part of an elite community. An investment in luxury yachts is not just a step towards wealth enhancement, but also a leap towards a lifestyle graced with elegance and grandeur.

Every market has its rhythm, a unique pulse - learning to ride the wave is the key. And remember, in the realm of luxury yachts, we are not just charting the course towards substantial financial returns, but also embarking on a journey that speaks the sophisticated language of richness.

Chapter 11. Building Wealth with High-End Real Estate Investments

High-end real estate, often synonymous with luxury and opulence, is a vibrant sector fostering wealth generation. This domain is not merely about acquiring homes; it signifies a strategic investment tool, solidifying investors' financial portfolios and magnifying their wealth acquisition strategies.

11.1. The Allure of High-End Real Estate

Luxury real estate properties are coveted totems for two significant reasons. Firstly, they provide a lavish lifestyle and secondly, they serve as excellent tools for financial investment. They thrive in prime locales, boasting exclusive amenities and stunning architecture aligned with magnificence and aesthetic appeal. From penthouses overlooking city skylines to sprawling mansions nestled amidst green expanses, high-end real estate combines luxury living with substantial returns.

This sector offers myriad opportunities for diversifying investment portfolios, promising potential appreciation in value over time. In addition to this, these properties can serve as excellent sources of rental income, enriching investors with a consistent, predictable revenue stream.

11.2. Understanding High-End Real Estate Market Dynamics

Before delving into high-end real estate, understanding the prevailing market dynamics is essential. Real estate markets, particularly luxury ones, are characteristically cyclical, affected by global economic events, interest rates, political stability, and stock market performance, among other factors.

Certain nuanced indicators are pertinent for spotting evolving markets. To name a few, these include looking at:

- Inventory levels: In a bucolic market, luxury properties tend to linger, elevating inventory levels.

- Months of supply: A market balanced between buyers and sellers usually has approximately six months of supply.

- Sales-to-list ratio: The percentage difference between the list price and final sale price; narrowing ratios signal a heating market.

A comprehension of these factors provides investors an analytical lens to evaluate potential investments, develop sustainable strategies, and forecast prospective changes in the market.

11.3. Recognizing Prime Locations

Location is paramount and a significant predictor of high returns in the luxury real estate sector. Premium properties are usually found in coveted neighborhoods and prestigious enclaves, areas well-connected to city centers, with excellent amenities and superior infrastructure.

Globally, various hotspots promise extravagant returns, ranging from Paris and New York City, characterized by their soaring skyscrapers and heritage townhouses, to the beachfront villas of Miami and Cannes, offering paradisaical views. These regions are immensely popular among the uber-rich, making them prime sites for high-end real estate investment.

Recognizing potential new zones of development, especially in rapidly urbanizing regions or areas attracting significant infrastructure investment, can also yield fruitful returns.

11.4. Capitalizing on Market Trends

Trending market shifts can catalyze the profitability of high-end real estate investments. For instance, the recent 'work from home' revolution, driven by the COVID-19 pandemic, has spiked interest in suburban and semi-rural properties, where buyers can access larger living spaces and solitude away from densely populated city centers.

Another emerging trend is the growing demand for sustainable, energy-efficient properties. 'Green luxury' is becoming increasingly coveted among affluent buyers focused on minimizing their environmental footprints. Properties that adhere to this philosophy – through the use of renewable energy sources, energy-efficient appliances, or sustainable materials – are becoming progressively attractive as investment options.

11.5. The Value of Property Management

Effectively managing a luxury property is as crucial as making the right investment decision. Property management encompasses a broad spectrum of operations such as maintenance, tenant management, tax handling, and dealing with legalities.

Many investors choose to hire professional property management companies to handle these complex nuances. These companies serve numerous functions, including finding and vetting prospective tenants, dealing with maintenance issues, collecting rentals, keeping abreast with relevant legislation, handling tax matters, and ensuring that the property is always in top condition.

11.6. Profiting from Luxury Rentals

Luxury rentals present an attractive opportunity to cash in on consistent, high-yield returns. Global tourists, corporate decision-makers, and affluent individuals often prefer luxury rentals for short-term stays, offering an alternative to commercial hospitality services. Catering to this niche market of high-paying tenants can prove significantly lucrative for luxury property investors.

11.7. The Power of Negotiation

Mastering negotiation skills can add significant premium to your high-end real estate investments. Whether dealing with brokers, sellers or renters, understanding the art of negotiation can help secure favorable deals and terms. This could include buying properties under market value, scoring well with rental prices, or getting better terms on your mortgage.

11.8. Utilizing Real Estate Investment Trusts (REITs)

Diversification in the high-end real estate sector can also be achieved with Real Estate Investment Trusts (REITs). REITs invest in income-generating properties and offer investors a way to access real estate markets without physically owning properties. This avenue provides exposure to a diversified portfolio of luxury properties, including residential estates, shopping centers, office buildings, and hotels among others, thereby expanding their investment repertoire and hedging against potential risks.

To sum up, high-end real estate serves as an excellent wealth-building tool. By comprehending market dynamics, identifying prime locations, capitalizing on market trends, managing properties efficiently, and leveraging negotiation and diversification tactics, investors can reasonably expect to amass significant wealth through luxury real estate investments. Harness the lustrous allure of high-end real estate, embrace the prospect of living and investing extravagantly, and let your wealth grow and glow!